Sportsviewers Guide
ATHLETICS

Simon Turnbull

DAVID & CHARLES
Newton Abbot   London

Contents

History and development   4–9
How the Olympics and modern athletics were derived from an Irish festival and the ancient Greek games.

Events and rules   10–15
All the disciplines of track and field are explained — from sprinting to throwing, from jumping to decathlon.

The track and equipment   16–17
A guide to electronic equipment, synthetic tracks and new technology.

The marathon   18–25
This special section analyses the latest running craze, with attention to the origins of the boom, the stars and the feel of the race.

The stars   26–43
Who's who in track and field, from Steve Cram to Allan Wells.

Cups and competitions   44–49
The new World championships have provided a rival to the Olympics as the greatest athletics meeting of all. Other major world, Commonwealth and European meetings are detailed.

Road to the top   50–53
How athletes prepare for a big race, through the long hours of training to the event itself, as seen through the eyes of Chris McGeorge, a Commonwealth Games bronze medallist.

Venues   54–57
A tour of major venues, from Bislett to Meadowbank, via Los Angeles.

People in the media   58–60
How the rival teams on BBC and ITV shape up on the starting blocks.

Statistics   61–63

British Library Cataloguing in Publication Data
Turnbull, Simon
   Athletics. — (Sportsviewers guides)
   1. Athletics — History
   I. Title   II. Series
   796.4′09   GV1060.3

ISBN 0-7153-8534-8

The Sportsviewers' Guide to Athletics was produced and designed by Siron Publishing Limited of 20 Queen Anne Street, London W1
Series editor: Nicholas Keith
Photographs by Tommy Hindley and Tony Henshaw of Professional Sport.
Designed by Ann Doolan

Typeset by ABM Typographics Ltd, Hull and printed by
Printer Industria Gráfica SA
Cuatro Caminos, Apartado 8,
Sant Vincenç dels Horts,
Barcelona, Spain DLB 36113-1983
for David & Charles (Publishers) Limited
Brunel House   Newton Abbot   Devon

Foreword

Why does the sport of athletics need a guide for television viewers? After all, athletics selects its winners in the most objective way — the fastest, highest and longest, so that's easy enough. Coupled with this is the undisputed fact that British television coverage of track and field events is by far the best — and most extensive — in the world.

However, Simon Turnbull's excellent efforts will be invaluable both to those who have only recently gained an interest in Britain's most successful major sport, and to those who have enjoyed its delights for many years. And how timely this publication is, following the first World Championships in Helsinki, which were seen by many millions around the world, and prior to the 1984 Olympics in Los Angeles, which will be seen by even more viewers.

Although track competitions are easily understood, most people have had little chance to learn about the skill events — the hurdles, jumps and throws — and the sophisticated technology which measures performances. All these aspects are explained, as are the rules, and the major competitions that take place around the world. The key venues are detailed, and the biographies of the personalities who will dominate our screens over the next few years are fascinating.

The platform of essential knowledge for all 'armchair spectators' is completed by well-researched sections on the history and development of the sport — of marathon running in particular — and with an 'athlete's-eye' view of preparation for a major competition.

You can also learn a little about those of us who put the words to the television pictures, and have therefore had the privilege to regularly see, travel with, and work with the great stars of our marvellous sport.

Good viewing!

Alan Pascoe MBE

3

History and development

The sport of track and field athletics, in the form we recognise it today, dates back little more than a century. But the roots of athletics history go back thousands of years.

Although most people believe the sport stems from the ancient Greek Olympic Games, the earliest athletics-based sports festival was the Taliteann Games, an annual thirty-day gathering held in County Meath, Ireland. Incorporating such events as foot racing and stone throwing, the games are thought to have been established in 1829 BC and survived until the Norman invasion in AD 1168.

There is a great deal of argument surrounding the origins of the Olympic Games, but positive documentary evidence of their existence dates back to 776 BC. They were staged in a four-yearly cycle at Olympia in southern Greece and survived until AD 393, when the Roman Emperor Theodesius abolished them by decree. The 'amateur' Olympic ideal was not introduced until the modern version of the games was founded towards the end of the nineteenth century: expensive gifts were awarded to the original Greek Olympic champions.

Rural sports meetings, which have prevailed since the Middle Ages, have also played a significant role in the development of athletics. Scottish Highland Games meetings were first held in the fourteenth century, and running, leaping and stone-casting were popular during the reign of Henry II (1154-1189). Stone-casting, a forerunner of shot putting, was such a widespread pastime during the reign of Edward III that he was forced to ban it in 1365 because it was preventing his militia from concentrating on archery practice.

An attempt to revise the Olympics was made by a London barrister, Robert Dover, in the seventeenth century. He organised the Cotswold

Games, which became known as Dover's 'Olympickes', but the idea of staging similar events did not spread and athletic activity throughout the following century was largely dominated by the growth of professional foot racing. Vast sums were wagered on the outcome of such 'pedestrian' races, usually held between rival footmen along turnpike roads.

Annual rural fairs, featuring running and throwing events, continued to flourish, but the seeds of modern amateur athletics were not sown until the upper classes started to become actively involved in athletic events. An annual sports day was held during the summer of 1812 at the Royal Military College, Sandhurst, and five years later the world's first athletics

club — the Neoton Guild — was formed in Norfolk. Athletics was soon added to the curriculum of public schools and made such an impression that the first university athletics meeting was held at Oxford in 1850.

The Amateur Athletic Club was formed in 1866 and organised annual national championships at the Little Bridge Athletic Ground in London. The club divided competitors into three separate classes of athlete: the professional, the gentleman amateur and the amateur. Professional and amateur athletes have been kept apart ever since; although it is ironic to note today that it was the AAC's aversion to the amateur athlete who worked for a living which led to its downfall.

The first Olympic Games 1896 (Mary Evans Picture Library).

Emil Zatopek: three golds in the 1952 Olympics. Here he leads Gordon Pirie in a 1955 race at the White City (Ed Lacey).

5

History and development/2

The club was eclipsed in 1880 when the universities of Oxford and Cambridge brought together the disparate amateur groups, which had developed throughout Britain, to form the Amateur Athletic Association. The AAA's strength gradually grew and, as the nineteenth century drew to a close, it was firmly established as the sole governing body of athletics in Britain.

By the turn of the century the modern Olympic Games had already taken their first faltering steps. Baron Pierre de Coubertin, a Frenchman greatly inspired by the ancient games and by the English public schools' sporting scene, persuaded a group of Greek businessmen to stage the first modern Olympic Games in Athens in March 1896. James Connolly, of the United States, won the triple jump with a leap of 13.71m to become the first modern Olympic champion. But, with only fifty-nine participating competitors, many of the world's leading athletes were missing.

It was not until the 1908 Olympics in London that the games began to take on a truly international look. The Olympic movement did not become firmly established until the 1912 games in Stockholm, by which time most competing nations had governing bodies — Sweden even employed a professional coach to prepare its Olympic team. That year marked the formation of the International Amateur Athletic Federation (IAAF), the supreme governing body controlling international athletics throughout the world. It was created to draw up and enforce rules and regulations on amateur definitions, and to recognise world records. It also formalised

6

Baron Pierre de Coubertin (2nd from left) with the Organising Committee for the first Olympic Games (BBC Hulton Picture Library).

the track and field events on the Olympic programme.

By the 1930s the Americans had emerged as the world's leading athletic nation. The American college system, with its widespread network of sports scholarships, produced an abundance of outstanding athletes, the best known of whom made his mark on world history as well as on the world record books. The 1936 Olympic Games in Berlin were supposed to be the showcase for Adolf Hitler's invincible Aryan race. Instead they became known as Jesse Owens' games. The black American won gold medals in the 100m, 200m, 4 × 100m and defeated the pride of the German team, Luz Long, to collect the long jump crown as well. A year ear-

lier, Owens had set six world records — 100 yards, long jump, 220 yards, 200m, 220 yards hurdles and 200m hurdles — within the space of forty-five minutes, while he was suffering from an injured back!

The rest of the world did not begin to catch up with the Americans until the 1950s. It was in 1950 that the Soviet Union first sent a team to the European championships. Two years later they confirmed their arrival as a world athletics force when they sent a well-trained team to the Helsinki Olympics. This team held its own in the men's events and dominated the women's programme.

The Soviets had analysed each event technically and developed new training methods. Following their initiative, Great Britain, France and West Germany began to develop organised coaching systems. The United States, however, were slow to

7

respond — probably because they were still winning the majority of Olympic medals.

The 1960 games in Rome were the first to be televised worldwide — and the subsequent growth in televised athletics slowly transformed the sport in the western world, generating interest, participation, sponsorship and much-needed money. With that new-found prosperity, however, came the problem of differentiating between amateur and professional athletes.

The term 'amateur' became inappropriate in the west because of undercover sponsorship and appearance money payments, while government support did likewise behind the Iron Curtain. East Germany's progression from 4 to 29 Olympic athletics medals between 1968 and 1980, for example, was largely due to a massive programme of state investment — in the form of coaching, research, facilities, sports medicine, food allowances, accommodation and work incentives — which resulted in a 2% drain on the national income.

The IAAF have recently taken steps to remove the hypocrisy of western athletes overcoming this advantage to east European athletes by changing the rules concerning amateurism. In 1982 they approved the setting up of trust funds, which allowed athletes to be openly paid for sponsorship and advertising deals. Twelve months later the IAAF agreed to the principle of appearance money being allowed in designated international invitation meetings (known as IAAF permit meetings).

'Monies accruing from sponsorship, advertising, and permit meetings are deposited in the athlete's trust fund (minus 15%, which goes to the athlete's national governing body as a handling fee). Athletes can draw from the trust fund to pay for coaching,

travelling expenses etc. and they receive the balance remaining in their fund when their careers come to an end.'

There have been a number of other significant developments in the last twenty-five years. The 1968 Olympics in Mexico were the first to be held on a synthetic track and now all major meetings take place on all-weather polyurethane surfaces. There has

been an alarming increase in the level of drug-taking at international level. Another development has been the growth of 'fun-running' and mass participation marathons.

The sport has certainly come a long way since the Taliteann Games. Yet the quintessence of athletics has remained the same. The basic drive to go faster, higher, further and the individualistic nature of the sport have always produced an endless line of outstanding champions and intriguing characters: from the feted heroes of the ancient games through to the Crams, Ovetts and Thompsons of today.

Coe and Ovett track the leader, East Germany's Jurgen Straub in the 1980 Olympic final of the 1500m. Cram, in white, is third from the left.

Events and Rules

The Sprints

The three sprint events contested at championship level are 100m, 200m and 400m. The most explosive of the running events, the sprints reduce running to its basic aim: the quest for maximum speed. The fastest speed officially recorded by an athlete is 27.89 miles an hour, which was achieved by the 1964 Olympic 100m champion, Bob Hayes, of the United States.

A key feature of all three sprints (and particularly of the 100m) is the start, which was revolutionised by the invention of starting blocks in 1927. Sprinters press their feet against two blocks — which are spaced apart and connected to a shaft — to improve their initial momentum. At major meetings starting blocks have an in-built electronic false-start detector, which indicates whether the athlete's feet leave the blocks earlier than they can be detected by the human eye.

Athletes are automatically disqualified after making two false starts. The starter gives two commands before starting sprint races: 'get to your marks', after which the athletes settle into their blocks; and 'set', upon hearing which the athletes raise their hips and knees off the ground and hold a crouched position for two or three seconds before the gun is fired.

The main features to look for in the sprinter's highly distinctive running action are the high knee-lift, the long strides, the thrusting arm action and the controlled breathing. Yet it would be misleading to give the impression that all three sprint races demand the same qualities. The start is crucial in the 100m, after which the athlete must build up to maximum speed as quickly as possible and hold form approaching the tape.

In the 200m, most top class sprinters attempt to 'coast' around the bend, maintaining top speed as effortlessly as possible, before driving hard for the line in the home straight. Pietro Mennea, of Italy, provided one of the most memorable examples of this technique when he overtook Allan Wells in the last 30m to win the Olympic title in 1980 after entering the final 100m next to last of the eight runners.

Pace distribution at the highest speed is even more important in the 400m. Many runners in the outside lanes have stormed around the opening 300m, only to be overtaken in the closing stages by rivals in the inside lanes. They have the considerable advantage of being able to see the competitors outside them.

Middle-distance

The events which fall into the 'middle-distance' category range from 800m to 3000m. In all middle-distance races, intermediate lap times are called out to the runners by track-side officials and a bell is rung as the runners enter the final lap.

A common feature of middle-distance races is the pushing, elbowing and tripping — usually unintentional — which is caused by the large number of runners taking part. Constant jockeying for position and bunching occur when the pace drops. In an attempt to avoid these incidents, the first bend of the 800m is run in lanes. As competitors pass the red flags at the beginning of the back straight, they break for the inside lane but will be disqualified if they cut inside too early.

Most international invitation middle-distance races include pacemakers — sometimes known as 'rabbits' — to ensure a fast time. Although such well-planned races are officially frowned on, two of the most famous world records — the mile times set by Roger Bannister in 1954 and by Sebastian Coe in 1981 — were accomplished with carefully orchestrated pacemaking.

Despite the advent of metrication, the mile has remained the 'blue riband' event of track and field athletics. The mid-1950s quest to break the four-minute mile barrier for four laps of the track helped to build up a challenging mystique around the event, which has been maintained by the perpetual drive to lower the record even further. Another major factor behind the mile's elevated standing has been the fact that it has been graced by many of the sport's all-time greats: from the fastest miler of the nineteenth century, Walter George: to his modern fellow-countrymen, Steve Ovett, Steve Cram and Sebastian Coe; not to mention famous Olympic champions such as Nurmi, of Finland (1924), Elliot, of Australia (1960), Snell, of New Zealand (1964) and Keino, of Kenya (1968) for the 1500m — otherwise known as the metric mile.

Long-distance

The three main long-distance events are 5,000m (12½ laps), 10,000m (25 laps) and the marathon (26 miles 385 yards). The marathon is examined in section seven. Stamina is the basic quality needed by a long-distance runner, but speed has also become an essential requirement for would-be world beaters. Even-paced runners such as Dave Bedford, the ebullient Briton, and the Australian Ron Clarke were superb world record breakers, but neither had the kind of acceleration needed to win major races.

Most top-class long distance races

Dick Fosbury demonstrates his high jump 'flop' (Ed Lacey).

11

Events and rules/2

develop into tactical 'sit and kick' affairs: the leading bunch of runners, once established, will conserve their efforts for a desperate sprint to the line on the last lap. One notable exception occured in the European 5,000m final in 1974 when Brendan Foster powered his way to a famous victory by employing 'kick and sit' tactics. He built up a commanding lead after injecting a fast pace in the middle of the race and then did enough to hold on over the remaining laps to collect the gold medal.

Twenty-four years earlier Emil Zatopek, of Czechoslovakia, captured the European 5,000m title and he can claim to be one of the greatest distance runners. Zatopek did not possess abnormal natural ability but, through his capacity for training harder and longer than anyone else had previously attempted, he set world records at distances between 5,000m and 10,000m. He is remembered most of all for his remarkable achievements at the 1952 Olympics in Helsinki, where he won gold medals for the 5,000m, 10,000m and the marathon.

3,000m steeplechase
The 3000m steeplechase comprises twenty-eight hurdles and seven water jumps, all three feet high. The need to clear them smoothly, without breaking the running rhythm, means that the steeplechase is not the 'soft option' for failed flat runners it is often made out to be.

Hurdles

The hurdles race distances are 110m and 400m for men, and 100m and 400m for women. There are ten hurdles in each of the men's events; the 110m hurdles being 3ft 6in (1.067m) high and the 400m hurdles 3ft (0.914m). The women's 100m hurdles is run over eight flights of 2ft 9in (0.84m), and there are ten 2ft 6in (0.762m) hurdles in the women's 400m event.

The main aim of hurdling is to clear the barriers quickly and efficiently, with the minimum of interruption to the running action — time spent in the air is time wasted. The hurdling technique involves a fast step-over action of the leading leg, followed by a sideways swing of the rear (take-off) leg, lifting only as high as is necessary to clear the barrier and get back into sprinting action as quickly as possible. Competitors are not disqualified for knocking down the hurdles, as long as it is not a blatantly deliberate act, but the trailing of a leg beside the hurdle is not allowed.

Relays

Relays are normally 4 × 100m and 4 × 400m races, between two or more teams of four athletes, who run the same distance in turn, passing a hollow metal baton (of approximately one foot in length). The baton must not be dropped and it has to be exchanged within a 20m 'take over' zone. Relay races are run in lanes, apart from the last three stages of the 4 × 400m, where teams can break for the inside lane on the back straight of the second runner's lap. Otherwise, competitors are not allowed to set foot in anyone else's lane.

Jumping

Long jump
Competitors can begin their jumps anywhere before the take-off board, but if they step over the edge and make spike marks in the plasticine strip immediately in front of the board the jump will not be considered legal. Jumps are measured from the break made in the sand by any part of the athlete's body or limbs nearest the take-off line.

12

Speed on the runway is most important and, after taking off from the board, long jumpers employ one of two main techniques in mid-air. Some jumpers try to put in an extra stride — which is known as the 'hitch-kick' — while others hang momentarily and then swing their arms and legs violently forward before landing.

The long jump competition at the 1968 Olympic Games in Mexico produced a phenomenal leap, which is widely accepted as the greatest single athletic feat of all time. It had taken thirty years for the world record to creep up from 8.13m (by Jesse Owens in 1935) to 8.35m before the lanky American Bob Beamon leapt an astonishing 8.90m in the rarified air of Mexico City. Beamon's best competitive jump before the Games had been 8.33m and his best afterwards was 8.20m—although he was said to approach his world record in practice.

Tessa Sanderson about to launch a javelin.

Triple jump
Known to many youngsters as 'the hop, step, and jump', the triple jump consists of three distinct phases. Competitors take off on one foot, land on the same foot (the hop), then take a long step to land on the other foot (the step) before landing on both feet in the sand-pit to complete the jump. The triple jumper needs less height than a long jumper when he hits the take-off board — if he goes too high on the hop phase, he will lose speed for the step.

High jump
The high jump competition is based on the extremes of success or failure. An athlete can have unlimited success, but three consecutive failures at a given height result in elimination. The winner is the last athlete remaining in the competition. If one or more people tie (fail at the same height), the winner is decided on 'countback': the jumper with the fewest failures.

Walking off to happiness: Ernesto Canto (Mexico) on his way to victory in the 1983 World Championships.

13

There are two main styles employed in high jumping: the straddle and the Fosbury flop. In the straddle, the jumper drapes himself across the bar face-downwards, rotating his body lengthways around it. The 'flopper' goes over the bar backwards, head first, lifting his legs up as the upper part of his body dips over the bar. The flop was originated by an American, Dick Fosbury, who began experimenting with the jump at the age of sixteen and honed it to perfection within five years to win the 1968 Olympic title.

Pole vault

The aim in the pole vault is to lever yourself over the cross-bar after approaching the vaulting box on a 40m runway and planting the pole into a box sunk in the ground underneath and just in front of the bar. The vaulter lets go of the pole, which is usually made of fibre-glass, at the moment of clearance and lands on a foam-rubber landing bed. This is a relatively new refinement, replacing the old sand beds, and has undoubtedly helped vaulters go even higher.

Knocking off the bar, placing the lower hand above the upper, moving the upper hand higher up the pole and touching the ground beyond the vertical with the bar all result in failure. If a pole breaks during an attempted vault it is not judged to be a failure. As in the high jump, competitors are eliminated after three failures at any height.

Throwing

Shot put

The shot is delivered from a concrete throwing circle and must land within a 40-degree sector. At the front end of the throwing circle is a 10cm high 'stop board', which helps prevent the thrower toppling forwards and out of

Lining up for a relay change.

the circle. The competitor is allowed to touch the inside of the 'stop board', but a foul is registered if he or she touches the top or outside. The shot must not be thrown; it is 'put' from the shoulder, with only one hand. The men's shot weighs 16lb (7.257kg) and the women's shot 8lb 13oz (4kg).

Discus

The discus is a spherical wooden implement, resembling a tiny flying saucer in shape. As in the shot, the discus is thrown from a concrete throwing circle and to be registered as valid must land within a 40-degree sector. A foul is recorded when a competitor has stepped into the circle and started to throw but touches the ground outside the circle or the top edge of the circle with any part of the body.

Unlike the shot (which is 'put' with a shuffling type of action from the back to the front of the circle), the discus is thrown after the athlete rotates his body around the circle three or four

must land within a 40-degree sector. The thrower rotates in the circle, spinning the hammer around him, before throwing it through an angled plane — low at the back, high at the front.

Decathlon

The decathlon, the men's multi-event competition, consists of four track and six field events. It is held on two consecutive days. First day 100m, long jump, shot, high jump and 400m. Second day 110m hurdles, discus, pole vault, javelin and 1500m. Competitors are allowed three attempts in the long jump and in the throwing events and are allowed to make two false starts in the sprint events.

Athletes must start in all ten events or they are considered to have abandoned the competition and will not figure among the final classification. Placings in the competition are determined by the total number of points scored by each competitor according to the IAAF scoring tables. The points range from 1 to 1,200 for each event. It is possible for an athlete to win the decathlon without finishing first in any event.

Heptathlon

The seven-event heptathlon replaced the five-event pentathlon at the start of the 1981 season as the standard multi-event competition for women. First day: 100m hurdles, shot, high jump, 200m. Second day: long jump, javelin, 800m.

Walking

Walkers must have one foot on the ground at all times or they are disqualified for 'lifting'. The curious, wiggling hip action is to allow full extension of the leg — another requirement of the rules. Only road races over 20 and 50km appear in the Olympics.

times. Discus — and hammer — circles are surrounded (apart from the front throwing sector) by a wire cage, to prevent implements flying into the crowd or on to the track.

Javelin
The javelin consists of three parts: a pointed metal head, a wooden or metal shaft, and a cord grip. It is thrown from a running approach and must be delivered over the shoulder or upper part of the throwing arm. It must not be slung or hurled, and at no time during the throw can the athlete turn around with his back towards the throwing arc. A throw is not valid unless the tip of the metal head strikes the ground before any other part of the javelin. The aim is to flight the javelin — too high or too low a trajectory will cause it to fall short.

Hammer
The hammer has a spherical metal head, a spring-steel wire and a grip. It is thrown from a concrete circle and

The Track and Equipment

The standard athletics track is a 400m (approx 437 yards) circuit. The 100m sprint and 100m and 110m hurdles races are run over the straight track in front of the main stand. All other races are run anti-clockwise around the track. The same finishing line is used for all races.

Running shoes

Eight lanes are marked on the track, to separate competitors and help avoid collisions. In races which start on a bend (200m and 400m), staggered starting lines are used. It may look as though some athletes are starting ahead of their rivals, but the stagger counteracts the effect of running wide round the bend and ensures that each athlete starts at an identical distance from the finishing line.

Electric timing is used at all top meetings, to avoid the inaccuracy of hand-timing. The timing device is started automatically, by a connection to the starter's pistol, and the results can be read from the photo-finish picture to the nearest one-hundredth of a second. In events up to 400m, only performances recorded by a fully automatic electronic timing device can be considered for world records. Apart from the mile, world records are recognised only over metric distances.

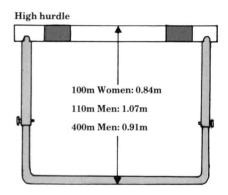

High hurdle

100m Women: 0.84m

110m Men: 1.07m

400m Men: 0.91m

In sprint and hurdles events up to 200m, as well as the triple jump and long jump, wind speed is measured by a special gauge. If the following wind is blowing at more than two metres per second, performances are classified as 'wind assisted' and cannot therefore be considered for record purposes.

Athletic performances have been revolutionised by the progression from grass to cinder to synthetic tracks: a fact which was emphasised beyond doubt at the 1968 Olympics in Mexico. Although high altitude was certainly a significant factor, the introduction of a synthetic track helped to create some phenomenal world records especially in the men's 100m, 400m and long jump.

Britain currently boasts some 60 synthetic tracks, while France has over ten times that number. There are many different types of synthetic tracks, but the most common ones laid are Tartan, Olymprene, Chevron, Mondo, Polytrack, Resisport, Polyflex, Rekortan.

Other improvements in equipment which have greatly assisted athletes are soft landing beds for pole vault and high jump; fibre-glass poles for vaulters and specially designed shoes for jumpers and road runners.

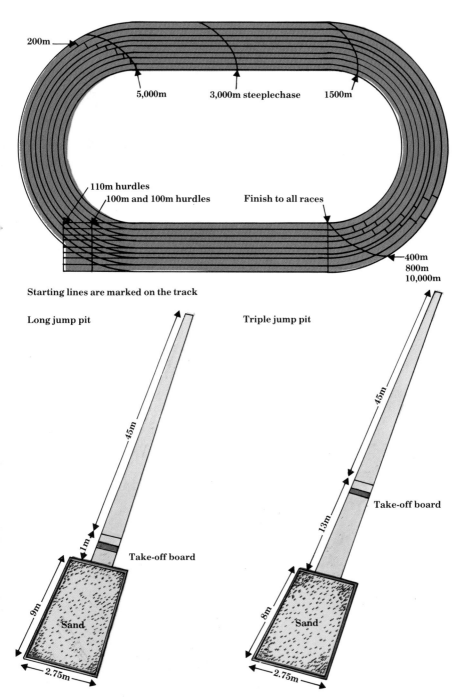

200m

5,000m 3,000m steeplechase 1500m

110m hurdles
100m and 100m hurdles Finish to all races

400m
800m
10,000m

Starting lines are marked on the track

Long jump pit

Triple jump pit

45m

45m

13m

Take-off board

1m

Take-off board

9m

8m

Sand

Sand

2.75m

2.75m

17

The Marathon

One of the most dramatic developments in recent athletics history has been the phenomenal rise in popularity of marathon running. The statistical facts alone are impressive. The total number of marathons held in the UK in 1978 was seventeen. Two years later there were still only 33, but in 1982 the figure rose to 130.

Only a few years ago the image of athletics in Britain was of Ovett and Coe rewriting the world record book on the running tracks of Europe. Now, it has been changed by the sheer volume of people taking to the streets of Britain in search of mental and physical fitness, and filled with the burning desire to complete the classic 26 miles 385 yards distance. The marathon boom has not only made a lasting impression on the record books but has — perhaps more importantly — broken down the barrier separating the average man on the street and the great athletic star.

Two important factors behind the boom have been the increasing public drive for health and fitness and a natural response to the running boom which swept the United States in the late 1970s. There is also the challenge of tackling an event which has always been surrounded by a mystical aura.

Only five years ago most people believed that the marathon was for super-fit athletes, who sometimes failed to complete the race themselves. But that misconception has been swept aside with the realisation that anyone can run a marathon at their own pace. It is no longer a race for the élite runner. Indeed, it is hardly a *race* at all for the vast majority in most big marathons.

Dorando Pietri gets a helping hand over the finishing line in the marathon, Olympic Games 1908 (BBC Hulton Picture Library).

18

The marathon/2

Origins and heroes

The origins of the marathon date back to 490 BC when Pheidippedes, a Greek soldier, ran from Marathon to Athens to convey the news that the Athenians had defeated their Persian invaders in a bloody battle. He collapsed and died at the gates of the Greek capital.

Who said that long distance running was lonely?

To the victor the spoils: Robert de Castella, the 1983 world marathon champion.

The same 25 mile route was used 2,386 years later for the marathon race at the first modern Olympic Games. The race was won by a Greek water carrier, Spiridon Louis, who had built up tremendous stamina running 14km each day alongside his mule, on which he carried water from his home village to sell in Athens. His reward for winning the race (in 2 hours 58 minutes 50 seconds) — from King George I — was a horse and cart, to ease his daily journey.

The official marathon distance of 26 miles 385 yards was set at the 1908 Olympics in London. The course, from Windsor Castle to the White City Stadium, measured 26 miles but competitors were required to cover an additional 385 yards of the track so they would finish opposite the Royal Box. That race produced one of the most dramatic finishes in the history of athletics.

Dorando Pietri, a tiny Italian, entered the stadium with a clear lead, but he collapsed several times on the track and was disqualified after being helped across the finish line by officials. Competitors are not allowed to be physically assisted during the race.

The 1954 Commonwealth marathon in Vancouver featured a similarly dramatic climax. The Englishman Jim Peters entered the stadium fifteen minutes ahead of his nearest rival but collapsed in the heat. After taking eleven agonising minutes to cover 185 yards of the track, and with only 200 yards left to run, officials mercifully carried him away.

The most famous marathon runner of all time is the Ethiopian Abebe Bikila. Unheard of outside his own country before the 1960 Olympics in Rome, he won the marathon in a world-best time of 2 hours 15 minutes 6.2 seconds — in bare feet! Four years later, at the Tokyo Games, he became the first man to retain the marathon title when he shattered his own Olympic record by three minutes; just five weeks earlier he had undergone an operation for appendicitis. In 1969 Bikila was seriously injured in a car crash and was confined to a wheelchair until he died, at the age of 41, in 1973.

The tenacious Australian, Rob de Castella, laid claim to being the world's number one marathon runner when he defeated his arch-rival, Alberto Salazar, of the United States, in the 1983 Rotterdam city marathon. Ever since de Castella came within

The marathon/3

five seconds of Salazar's world record (2 hours 8 minutes 13 seconds, which he set in the 1981 New York marathon) in Japan's Fukuoka marathon in December 1981, arguments had raged as to who was truly the world's greatest marathon runner.

Salazar arrived in the Netherlands with an unbeaten marathon record, the world record, and a clear edge in terms of basic speed, whereas de Castella had impressively won the Commonwealth title from Tanzania's Juma Ikangaa in October 1982. While Salazar trailed home fifth in 2 hours 10 minutes 8 seconds, de Castella held off a surprise challenge from Portugal's Carlos Lopes to win by two

seconds in 2 hours 8 minutes 37 seconds.

The race was an exciting prelude to the clash between de Castella and Salazar in the 1984 Los Angeles Olympics. But the performance of

Abebe Bikila collects the marathon gold medal, Tokyo 1964 (Ed Lacey).

Alberto Salazar

Grete Waitz

Lopes, completing a marathon for the first time at the age of 36, underlined the emergence of another great long-distance runner. Lopes, a Lisbon bank clerk who won a silver 10,000m medal behind Lasse Viren at the 1976 Olympics, returned from injury in style in the early months of 1983. As well as his outstanding Rotterdam run, he finished second in the World cross-country championships — ahead of both de Castella and Salazar — and missed breaking the world 10,000m record only by a second during the early part of the track season.

Grete Waitz (née Anderson) is the world's greatest women's marathon and long-distance runner. The slender Norwegian took over two minutes off the previous world best by clocking 2 hours 32 minutes 30 seconds on her marathon début, in the 1978 New York marathon. In the 1979 New York race she reduced her record to 2:27:33 and returned to the 'Big Apple' twelve months later to record 2:25:42.

In 1981 she lost her New York title to New Zealand's Alison Roe, after pulling out of the race at 15 miles suffering from injury; Roe went on to set a new record of 2 hours 25 minutes 29 seconds. Waitz, who has also set world records at 3,000m and 10,000m, seemed to be on the decline when she lost the World cross-country championships in March 1982. But she won the cross-country crown for the fifth time in March 1983, a month before equalling Roe's world marathon record in the London marathon. The day after the London race, however, a little-known American Joan Benoit took three minutes off the record with an astonishing time of 2 hours 22 minutes 43 seconds in the Boston marathon. However, Waitz was a comfortable winner of the marathon in the World championships in August 1983, when Benoit did not compete.

The feel of a marathon

References to the marathon as a 'fun-running' event have tended to obscure the fact that, for serious competitors, the marathon is still as gruelling today as it was in the days of Dorando Pietri and Jim Peters. The worst aspect of marathon running for top class international runners is the process of 'hitting the wall' — which usually occurs between 18-22 miles, when the body's supply of glycogen (the energy source stored in the muscles) has been used up. While the body switches to fat for its fuel, the runner suddenly feels drained and may slow dramatically, which comes so unexpectedly it quite literally feels like running into a wall.

The marathon is certainly not fun at international level,' says Rob de Castella. 'You have to develop a mental ability to ignore pain. If you let the pain overcome you, you might as well have not bothered entering. You have to immerse yourself in total concentration and, if you get it right, the concentration should tend to outweigh the pain and exhaustion. The hard part is keeping that concentration going for the whole duration of the race.

The inaugural Gillette London marathon — organised by Britain's 1956 Olympic 3,000m steeplechase champion Chris Brasher — in March 1981 signalled the start of the boom in Britain. With over 7,000 competitors, it was (at the time) Britain's biggest race. There were 16,350 runners in the following year's race.

While Britain's top marathon is still in its infancy, America's two main marathons, at Boston and New York, have been held since the latter years of the nineteenth century. Other leading international marathons include: Fukuoka (Japan), Kosiche (Czechoslovakia), Enschede (Netherlands) and Athens (Greece).

Joan Benoit

The Stars

One of the main features of athletics over the years has been the unrelenting flow of outstanding champions. Today is no exception. There are many brilliant champions and record holders — and this chapter is devoted to twelve of the most outstanding of today's world stars.

Eamonn Coghlan
(Republic of Ireland)
The curious spectacle of Eamonn Coghlan doing what appeared to be an Irish jig as he rounded the final turn during the 1983 World championships 5,000m final will go down as one of the most poignant sights in modern athletics. In the mid-1970s the amiable Irishman established himself as one of the world's greatest indoor runners, drawing huge crowds to the massive American indoor stadia to witness his annual world record breaking feats. Each year, Coghlan was expected to produce his phenomenal indoor form outdoors. But outdoor world records and titles eluded him.

He was overhauled in the home straight of the Olympics 1500m final in 1976, finishing just out of the medals in fourth place, the position he also filled in similar style over 5,000m in the Moscow Olympics four years later. Sandwiched in between his two 'Olympic failures' came Coghlan's only major medal success before 1983 — his second place in the European 1500m final of 1978. But, even then, many critics argued that the manner in which he happily settled for the silver medal behind Steve Ovett underlined the absence of the killer instinct needed by a true champion.

So Coghlan arrived in Helsinki for the 1983 World championships knowing he had only two more chances of claiming a major title (the other, of course, being in the 1984 Olympics). This time he made no mistakes. As the

In heaven: Eamonn Coghlan after his victory in the 1983 World Championship 5,000m final.

challenge from the reigning European champion and pre-race favourite, Thomas Wessinghage, evaporated when the Russian Dmitry Dmitriyev injected a telling burst on the pen-ultimate lap, Coghlan gradually clawed back the Russian's lead. He drew level in the last 200m, looked over his shoulder to see nobody within striking distance and realised he had the race sewn up.

Coghlan clenched his fists, raised his arms and almost jumped for joy before looking into his rival's face. It could have been taken for an unsport-ing and arrogant gesture from any other athlete, but not from Eamonn Coghlan. After seven years of getting it wrong when it mattered, he had at last 'cracked it' — and he sped clear off the final bend to complete one of the most fully savoured major champion-ship victories of all time.

Sebastian Coe (GB)
Sebastian Coe first emerged as a world-class runner in 1977 when, at the age of 20, he won the European indoor 800m title. A year later, Coe con-firmed his arrival on the world scene by claiming third place — behind Olaf Beyer and Steve Ovett — in the 800m final of the European championships in Prague, but it was in 1979 that the elegant Loughborough University student etched his name permanently into the annals of world athletics.

Within the space of forty-one days he captured three of the most prized world records: 800m (1 min 42.4 secs), the Mile (3 mins 49.0 secs) and 1500m (3 mins 32.1 secs). It was a remarkable record-breaking spree which installed Coe as the firm favourite for both the 800m and the 1500m gold medals at the 1980 Olympics in Moscow.

27

Sebastian Coe contemplates the future.

After setting a world 1,000m record of 2 mins 13.4 secs in Oslo, he was beaten in the 800m Olympic final by his arch-rival, Steve Ovett, and had to settle for the silver medal. The odds then shifted in Ovett's favour for the 1500m, but Coe bounced back in dramatic style to claim the gold medal ahead of the East German Jurgen Straub and Ovett.

In 1981 Coe turned his attention to the record books again, beginning his season by setting a remarkable world 800m record of 1 min 41.72 secs and lowering his 1,000m mark to 2 mins 12.8 secs. Then followed an astonishing nine-day battle for the world mile record with Ovett — who had lowered it to 3 mins 48.8 secs before the Moscow Olympics. First Coe reclaimed it with a 3 min 48.53 secs run in Zurich; Ovett ran 3 mins 48.4 secs in Koblenz the following week and Coe regained it 48 hours later with a time of 3 mins 47.33 secs in Brussels.

In 1982 Coe recovered from a stress bone fracture — which ruled out a triple confrontation with Ovett over 800m, 1500m and 3,000m — and lined up as a strong favourite to gain his first ever major 800m medal at the European championships in Athens. Taking the lead off the final bend, Coe looked destined for victory, but he tired up badly, was overtaken by an unfancied West German, Hans-Peter Ferner.

Two days later, it was diagnosed that the London-born runner was suffering from glandular fever and, although he returned to the European circuit in 1983, a recurrence of the illness forced him to abandon his bid to win the world 800m title less than a week before the opening of the World championships in Helsinki, following four bad defeats in five races. Coe, who is coached by his father, Peter, must now reassess his mental and physical approach to running.

Keith Connor (GB)

Keith Connor, Britain's greatest ever triple jumper, is not entirely a product of the British athletics system. Born in Anguilla, West Indies, Keith took up athletics as a youngster in Slough and then moved to Wolverhampton to link up with his present coach, Ted King, but the foundations of his world-class career were formed in the United States, where he has studied at the University of El Paso and the Southern Methodist University.

He burst on to the international scene at the age of 20 in 1978 by collecting a silver medal at the European indoor championships and then winning the Commonwealth title in Edmonton, Canada. At the Moscow Olympics in 1980, he was disappointed to finish just out of the medals in fourth place, but two years later he became firmly established as the world's leading triple jumper.

Keith Connor

Early in the 1982 season he became the second longest triple jumper in history and claimed the European and Commonwealth records with a leap of 17.57m, before winning the European and Commonwealth gold medals. Favourite for the world title in 1983, he was hit by an ankle injury and created a major shock on the opening day of the championships by being eliminated in the qualifying rounds.

Steve Cram (GB)

While the media's attention was focused on the battle for world middle-distance running supremacy between Steve Ovett and Sebastian Coe, Steve Cram gradually and quietly became accustomed to life at the top of the athletics tree. In 1982 and 1983, as Ovett and Coe slipped from their perch, the young Jarrow runner emerged as the world's leading middle-distance runner.

He was 'discovered' at the age of 12 at a Tyneside schools meeting by Jimmy Hedley, his coach at the time, and this tall, gangling runner with the long, raking stride first ran for England five years later in the Commonwealth Games in Edmonton in 1978. Two years later, he clinched the third 1500m place in Britain's Olympic team (alongside Ovett and Coe) and gained valuable experience by finishing eighth in the final. In 1982 he started to emerge from the shadows of Ovett and Coe, displaying clinical tactical awareness to win both the European and Commonwealth titles, and also topping the world rankings for 800m. But Ovett and Coe had not been among his 'victims' in 1982 and another twelve months passed before Cram's enormous talent began to be fully appreciated.

At the start of the 1983 season ten weeks of injury problems and missed training threatened to wipe out his

summer, but — only three weeks after his first race of the season — he became the first British runner for ten years, other than Steve Ovett, to beat Sebastian Coe over 800m. Two weeks later he ran a perfect tactical race in the World championship 1500m final to win the gold medal.

In September 1983, Cram confirmed

Steve Cram on Mike Boit's shoulder in Helsinki.

his place at the very top by beating Ovett in a mile race at Crystal Palace. Remarkably, Cram has no coach, but his immense calm and inner confidence should keep him at the top for many years to come — barring unforeseen injury.

Mary Decker (US)

Mary Decker was an international star at the age of fourteen. In 1973 she toured the world with the US track team and hit the headlines by defeating Russia's Olympic silver 800m medallist Niole Sabaite in Minsk. A year later, although still only 15, she set a world indoor 880 yards best, but

31

Mary Decker

her expected progress received a set-back in her later teens.

Training hard during growth periods almost crippled her and it took her four years to overcome several operations and return to action. In 1978 she set a world indoor 1,000 yards best and captured her first international title twelve months later when she won the 1500m final at the Pan-American Games in Puerto Rico.

After setting a world mile record, Mary would have been one of the favourites to win the same title at the

Marita Koch

1980 Moscow Olympics, but her hopes of Olympic glory were dashed by the American boycott. Three years later, however, she took on the fast-finishing Russians at the World championships in Helsinki.

In the 3,000m final she dispensed with her usual tactic of trying to break the field from early on and two Russian girls, Svetlana Ulmasova and Tatyana Kazankina, were both poised ominously on her shoulder with 100m left. When Kazankina edged ahead in the home straight, Mary's chances of gold seemed to be disappearing, but she produced a startling sprint finish to win the title. The 1500m proved a remarkably similar affair, with Mary claiming victory in the last few strides after the Russian Zamira Zaitseva seemed to have clinched the race by overtaking her in the final 200m.

Marita Koch (East Germany)
Perhaps the most celebrated female athlete of the last decade, Marita Koch first emerged as a threat to Irena Szewinska's domination of women's 400m running in 1977 when, at the age of 20, she won the European indoor crown and triumphed in the Europa Cup final. She then fought a terrific duel with Szewinska in the 1977 World Cup final in Düsseldorf, losing to the 'Polish princess' by less than a quarter of a second.

But only another twelve months elapsed before she eclipsed Szewinska. After twice breaking the world 400m record and setting new figures for 200m, she set her fourth world record of the year in the European championships to take the gold medal in 48.94 secs and thus became the first woman to break the 49 second barrier. In 1979 she emulated the record-smashing feats of Sebastian Coe by twice breaking her world 200m record (22.02 secs and 21.71 secs) and doing likewise in the one-lap event (48.89 secs and 48.6 secs) before winning the Olympic title in Moscow in 1980.

The Olympic final marked the beginning of the end of the medical student's undisputed domination of the women's 400m scene. For, only two strides behind her, the powerfully-built Czech runner, Jarmila Kratochvilova, marked her rapid improvement by winning the silver medal.

A year later, at the World Cup final in Rome, Kratochvilova missed the world record by only one-hundredth of a second, whereas Koch — returning from a long spell of injury — finished a well-beaten second. It was her first 400m defeat since 1977. But in September 1982 Koch gained revenge in the European championships, winning the gold medal in a new world record time of 48.16 seconds.

After losing a great deal of endurance training through injury, Koch chose to concentrate on 100m and 200m at the 1983 World championships. She finished second to her fellow East German, Marlies Göhr, in the shorter event and claimed the gold ahead of Jamaica's Merlene Ottey in the 200m, but her sweetest triumph in Helsinki came in the 4 × 400m relay. With the opposing teams expecting her not to compete, she surprisingly ran the third leg to give the East Germans a commanding lead. Even Kratochvilova (who set a world 400m record of 47.99 seconds in the individual final) could not bridge the gap on the final leg.

Carl Lewis (US)

Universally hailed as 'the new Jesse Owens', Carl Lewis first rocked the world athletics scene in 1981. During that summer, at the age of 19, he clocked the fastest ever 100m time at sea level and came within 27cm of Bob Beamon's 'untouchable' world long jump record — 8.9m (29ft 2½in) set in the 1968 Olympics at altitude in Mexico — with a marginally wind-assisted leap of 8.63m.

Lewis began his magnificent 1983 season by achieving something which eluded even the great Owens — three individual wins at the US championships. After winning the 100m, he leaped 8.79m in the long jump — the best ever at sea-level and second on the world all-time list — and, despite waving to the crowd and easing up well before the line, he took the 200m in 19.75 seconds, the best ever 200m run at sea-level and a mere three-hundredths of a second outside Pietro Mannea's world record.

Lewis went on to complete another famous 'hat-trick' at the inaugural World championships in Helsinki. He became the star of the strongest ever athletics championship by winning gold medals in the 100m and long jump and anchoring the US team to victory in the 4 × 100m relay.

Sport runs in the Lewis family. Carl's mother, Evelyn, was an international sprint hurdler; his father, Bill, is a sports teacher and lecturer in sociology; his sister, Carol, is an international long jumper and his brother, Cleve, was among the first black soccer players when he joined the Memphis Rogues in late 1979.

Dave Moorcroft (GB)

On 7 July 1982, Dave Moorcroft produced one of the greatest runs ever in the history of sport. Henry Rono's world 5000m record had been regarded as one of the best in the books until Moorcroft turned in an astonishing display of front-running at the Oslo Games to shatter it by six seconds and leave Rono half a lap behind. In doing so, the 29 year-old Coventry runner missed breaking the 13 minute barrier by a mere 0.42 of a second.

Only a few months earlier Moorcroft had undergone a calf operation, which could have brought an end to his international career. Despite being an Olympic 1500m semi-finalist in 1976 and winning the Commonwealth metric mile title two years later, he had to live in the shadows of Steve Ovett and Sebastian Coe and decided to move up to 5,000m for the 1980 Olympics. A bout of 'Moscow tummy trouble' caused him to bow out in the semi-finals, but he bounced back in 1981 to win the European Cup final 5,000m.

Following his world record in Oslo he could finish only third in the 1982 European championships, but atoned for that disappointment by winning the Commonwealth 5,000m title a month later. The 'up and down' story of his career continued in 1983 when hepatitis and two stress fractures on his right foot ended his track season, although he appeared for an outing in the autumn and seemed none the worse for wear, winning a 3,000m race at Jarrow. Coached by John Anderson, Moorcroft and his wife, Linda, have a son.

Ed Moses (US)

Edwin Moses, the smooth-hurdling American, first turned his attention to the 400m hurdles in 1975 when he clocked a promising, but scarcely earth-shattering time of 52.0 seconds. A year later, at 20, he broke John Akii-Bua's world record with the time of 47.64 seconds he produced to win the Olympic gold medal in Montreal by the crushing margin of eight metres.

He would almost certainly have collected his second Olympic gold in Moscow, but was absent because of the American boycott. While many of his fellow countrymen moaned about their lost Olympic chances, Moses was driven to prove beyond doubt that he

Dave Moorcroft's golden moment in the 1982 Commonwealth Games 5,000m final.

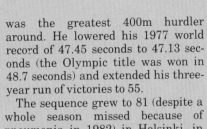

was the greatest 400m hurdler around. He lowered his 1977 world record of 47.45 seconds to 47.13 seconds (the Olympic title was won in 48.7 seconds) and extended his three-year run of victories to 55.

The sequence grew to 81 (despite a whole season missed because of pneumonia in 1982) in Helsinki, in August 1983, when he added the world title to his ever-growing list of triumphs. Not even a shoelace which became untied around the final bend could stop him from majestically flowing over the ten flights to finish in 47.5 seconds, 1.11 seconds ahead of the West German Harald Schmid (who, at a meeting in Berlin in August 1977, was the last man to beat him). Later in the season, he set a new world record of 47.02 seconds in Koblenz.

Ed Moses

37

Steve Ovett with his wife Rachel.

Steve Ovett (GB)

Steve Ovett's fourth place in the 1500m final at the 1983 World championships brought an (at least temporary) end to his reign as the world's leading mile/1500m competitor. His competitive record between 1977 and 1983 was second to that of no other runner: the 1978 European 1500m title, the 1980 Olympic bronze medal and the 1981 World Cup 1500m gold were just the tip of his achievements.

He took on all-comers in dozens of races and suffered less than a handful of defeats; the sight of him swooping past his opponents with 200m left and waving to the crowd on his way to victory became commonplace at top-class international meetings.

Despite his awesome record, Ovett lost his two most important 1500m races. After three gruelling 800m races and two tough 1500m rounds, he finished behind Sebastian Coe and Jurgen Straub in the 1980 Olympic 1500m final, thus bringing an end to a streak of 45 successive wins over 1500m and the mile. His reputation as one of the world's greatest tactical middle-distance runners was well and truly shattered three years later in the inaugural World championships when he allowed himself to become hopelessly boxed in at the bell and could not claw his way back to Steve Cram, Steve Scott and Said Aouita on the last lap.

Born and bred in Brighton, Ovett started as an 800m runner and has a far better championship record at the two-lap distance than Sebastian Coe. After winning the European junior 800m title in 1973, he took the silver medal at the distance at the following year's European championships when aged only 18.

Two years later he was bitterly disappointed at finishing only fifth in the Olympic final in Montreal and in 1978 he finished behind Olaf Beyer (but ahead of Sebastian Coe) to collect the European championships silver medal in Prague. But his most famous two-lap triumph came at the Moscow Olympics in 1980 when he totally upset the form book by winning the gold medal ahead of Coe.

Since setting a world two mile record in 1978, Ovett has gone out to break the world mile record twice and 1500m record three times; his latest triumph came at Reiti in Italy in September 1983 when he regained the world 1500m record from Sydney Maree with a time of 3 minutes 30.78 seconds.

Daley Thompson (GB)

Daley Thompson's decathlon triumph at the 1983 World championships proved beyond doubt that he is the greatest all-round athlete ever to grace the sport of track and field athletics. This fact has never been fully appreciated by a British sporting public which does not hold the ten-event decathlon in the same kind of esteem as the mile or 1500m.

That has been the case since, at the age of 18, he earned selection for the Montreal Olympics where he came eighteenth. Two years later he collected 8,467 points to win the Commonwealth title in Edmonton, Canada, but a poor pole vault cost him the gold medal at the European championships three weeks later and he had to settle for second place behind Russia's Aleksandr Grebenyuk.

In May 1980, in the small Austrian town of Gotzis, he not only beat the West German Guido Kratschmer (who, but for the West German boycott, would have been his main Olympic rival that year), but broke Bruce Jenner's four-year-old world record with a score of 8,622 points. Kratschmer himself broke Thompson's record a month later, but

Thompson comfortably won the Olympic title later in the summer.

He opened his outstanding 1982 campaign by reclaiming the world record in Gotzis with 8,704 points, but became injured and then saw the West German Jurgen Hingsen (whom he had beaten in Gotzis) set a new record of 8,723 points. The subsequent 'showdown' at the European championships in Athens was decidedly one-sided with Thompson taking the gold and adding 20 points to the world record. A month later he retained his Commonwealth title in Brisbane.

In June 1983 Hingsen reclaimed the world record by scoring 8,777 points during the West German World championship trials. Thompson, meanwhile, had been hit by back and groin injuries and was doubtful about competing in Helsinki until the night before the competition started. Although well below peak fitness, Thompson led all the way to beat Hingsen by 8,666 points to 8,561 points and thus become the first athlete ever to hold Olympic, World, European and Commonwealth titles at the same time.

Allan Wells (GB)

After starting his athletic life as a triple jumper and long jumper, Allan Wells did not turn his attention to .sprinting until he reached his mid-twenties. He was aged 26 when he broke Peter Radford's long-standing British record by clocking 10.15 seconds at the UK championships in his home town of Edinburgh in 1978. He confirmed his arrival as one of the world's leading sprinters when he captured the 200m title and finished second to Jamaica's Don Quarrie in the 100m.

Two years later the powerful Scot — who is coached by his wife Margot — capped a storybook rise to interna-tional prominence by winning the Olympic 100m title in Moscow. Wells came within a whisker of claimimg the coveted Olympic sprint 'double', being pipped on the line by the fast-finishing Italian Pietro Mennea in the 200m final.

Wells proved that his Olympic triumph was far from 'hollow' twelve months later when he defeated the top Americans — who had been absent from Moscow because of their boycott — to win the IAAF 'Golden Sprints' title in Cologne. In 1982 he continued to build on his impressive major championship record by winning the Commonwealth 100m title and dead-heating with Mike McFarlane for the 200m gold. A year later, though 31 and less fully fit, he claimed fourth place over 100m and 200m at the World championships in Helsinki. He returned to Britain a week later to gain a thrilling 200m victory over Mennea in the Europa Cup Final.

Pietro Mennea: world record breaker and 1980 Olympic champion at 200m.

Allan Wells

Cups and competitions

The inception of the IAAF World championships in 1983 was a significant development in the history of world athletics. The championships will rank behind only the Olympic Games in terms of prestige and most international athletes can now attempt to win a major title every year. Only a few years ago British athletes would have a 'build-up' or 'fallow' year in between the Olympic Games and, two years later, the European championships and Commonwealth Games. Now, the four-yearly championships cycle is: Olympic Games, World cup, European championships/Commonwealth Games, World championships.

Olympic Games

Whether or not the modern revival of the Olympic Games has been the most significant moulding influence on the shape of today's track and field athletics is open to debate. But there can be no doubting the fact that the Olympic Games are firmly established as the world's most prestigious athletics championships. From the moment a young child first begins to excel at any athletic event, the highest pinnacle is the winning of an Olympic gold medal.

The games have steadily grown since Baron Pierre de Coubertin's 1896 revival, when only 59 athletes from 10 countries contested the track and field events. At the 1972 games in Munich, 104 countries were represented; although the numbers fell to 78 in 1976 and 69 in 1980 because of political boycotts — a feature of the Olympics that has become as integral as the many outstanding champions who have emerged over the years.

The winner of the most Olympic athletics medals is the Finnish distance runner, Paavo Nurmi, who also set 29 world records during a glittering international career. He won 12 Olympic medals — 9 golds and 3 silvers — at the 1920, 1924 and 1928 Games. A subsequent 'Flying Finn', Lasse Viren, created Olympic history in 1976 at Montreal by retaining both the 5,000m and 10,000m titles (which he surprisingly won at the 1972 games). Apart from finishing third over 5,000m at the 1974 European championships, Viren — the bearded policeman — achieved little else of note during his running career.

World championships

Until 1983 the Olympic track and field events were officially termed 'world championships' by the IAAF. Thus, every winner of an Olympic title automatically became a world champion. But in 1983 the IAAF made one of the most significant developments in the history of athletics when they organised their first world championships in Helsinki. Now many great athletes, who may otherwise have ended their career without the supreme accolade of an Olympic gold medal, will have the opportunity to reduce that disappointment by earning the right to be called a world champion. The championships are to be held every four years, one year before the Olympics. The 1987 event is to be staged in Rome.

European Championships

The brainchild of a Hungarian, Szilard Stankovits, the European championships were first held in Turin in 1934 and have included both men's and women's events since 1946. The 1982 championships in Athens were the thirteenth. The elegant Polish sprinter, Irena Szewinska (née Kitszenstein), won a record total of ten European championship medals (including six golds). After winning silver medals in the long jump and 200m and a gold 4 x 100m relay medal

Lasse Viren, who achieved a unique "double double" in the Olympics.

Cups and competitions/2

Irene Szewinska wins the 1968 Olympic 200m final from Raelene Boyle (Ed Lacey).

on her Olympic début — as an eighteen-year-old in Tokyo — she went on to win the Olympic 200m title in 1972 and 400m in Montreal four years later.

wealth nations as on the winning of medals. The first British Empire Games (they were renamed the British Commonwealth Games in 1970) were held in Hamilton, Canada in 1930. The driving force behind them was a sports reporter on the Hamilton *Spectator*, Bobby Robinson, who had been Canada's athletics team manager at the 1928 Olympics. Women's events were introduced at the second games, in London in 1934. The 1986 Games in Edinburgh will be the thirteenth.

World Cup

The IAAF's inaugural World cup competition, held in Düsseldorf in 1977, was a resounding success — both as a major world athletics event and as a source of finance for the federation to divert towards the development of athletics in the Third World. The format of the world's strongest individual nations competing against continental teams proved immensely popular — with the world's leading athletes battling not only for their own honour, but for the pride of their nation or continent.

Although the second World cup in Montreal in 1979 was much less popular (attracting less than half of the Düsseldorf crowds), the 1981 event in Rome was another great success. The competition was temporarily suspended in 1983 because of the IAAF's decision to hold it once every four years instead of bi-annually in order to fit their World Championships into the athletics diary. The 1985 World Cup will take place in Canberra, Australia.

Commonwealth Games

Although one of the world's major athletics championships, the Commonwealth Games have been dubbed 'the friendly games', for the emphasis has been as much on the meeting of peoples from the British Common-

Europa (European) Cup

A European Cup, featuring qualifying semi-finals and one athlete per nation per event, was conceived by Bruno Zauli, a former president of the IAAF's European committee. The first

Cups and competitions/3

tournament was held in 1965 and the 1983 event at Crystal Palace marked the ninth year of competition; since 1973 it has been held on a two-year cycle. The pattern of winners between 1970 and 1981 underlined East Germany's firm grip on European athletics. During that period they failed to win only one of the fourteen trophies contested — they narrowly lost the women's competition to the Soviet Union in 1973.

European Indoor Championships

The major winter event for non-distance athletes in Europe, these championships have been held annually — usually in February or March — since 1966. They acted as a springboard to international stardom for Valery Borzov, the powerful Russian sprinter who has been the championships' most successful competitor. Borzov, who became the first European to land the coveted Olympic spring 'double' when he won the 100m and 200m at the 1972 Games, took the European indoor 50m or 60m title seven times between 1970 and 1977.

World Cross-country Championships

From parochial British origins, the World Cross-country Championships (formerly known as the International cross-country championships) have developed into the main athletics event of the winter. The first 'international' was staged between the four home countries in 1903 and the competition was dominated by England until it came under the jurisdiction of the IAAF in 1973, when it was renamed 'the IAAF World Cross-country Championships'. Since then, only one British runner — Ian Stewart, of Scotland — has won the men's individual title. More and more nations

Cram displays his Commonwealth 1500m gold medal.

have decided to take part and the Ethiopians have dominated the men's and junior men's races since they first entered the championships in 1981.

Jack Holden (England), Alain Mimoun (France) and Gaston Roelants (Belgium) have won the senior men's race four times. Holden and Jean Bouin (France) won the race in three successive years. Norway's Grete Waitz equalled the record set by Doris Brown, of the United States, when she collected the women's title for the fifth time at Gateshead in 1983.

British championships

Since its inception in 1880, the **AAA championships** have served as the unofficial British championships — although they are open to foreign competitors and despite the creation of the UK (closed) championships. The Trinidadian sprinter, Emmanuel McDonald Bailey, holds the record for winning the most AAA titles. Excluding relays, he won fourteen gold medals between 1946 and 1953. The Women's AAA, which was founded in 1922, hold their own separate championships. While the home of the AAA championships has been at Crystal Palace since 1970, the **UK closed championships** have been staged at a different venue each year since they were inaugurated by the British Amateur Athletic Board in 1977.

The **AAA indoor championships** have been staged at RAF Cosford, near Wolverhampton, since 1965. But the focal point of the winter in Britain is probably the **English national cross-country championships**, held over nine miles of testing (and usually muddy) terrain. With almost 2,000 club runners taking part, the championships carry a great deal of prestige among the British distance running fraternity and most of the top international distance runners attempt to win the coveted senior men's title.

49

Road to the top

Despite the significant rise in the popularity of athletics in recent years, most people watching international athletics meetings on television know very little about the kind of unseen work athletes must undergo to reach that level. Top athletes train at least twice a day (for between two to three hours) all year round — even when snow, rain and fog hampers those who need to do their training outdoors. It is a time-consuming, and quite often soul-destroying 'pastime' for amateur sportsmen, who also have to find the time to work for a living.

The content and intensity of training sessions vary considerably from event to event and from athlete to athlete. But, to give a better insight into the preparation of an international athlete, here are two days in the life of Chris McGeorge, an 800m runner (who, at the age of 20, won a bronze medal at the 1982 Commonwealth Games in Brisbane). He describes a typical day in his winter and the day which climaxed his year's training in 1982.

Winter slog

'I get up at 7am, do stretching exercises for fifteen minutes and then go for a five mile run with a friend. I'm lucky because I'm studying at Loughborough and there are plenty of other runners around to share the burden of training. That can be very important, especially in the winter when it can be a hard, soul-destroying grind.

There are many days when you have so many other pressures and are completely disillusioned — it's raining or snowing; you've got essays to do for college; you're exhausted; or you're not running or feeling very well. Everything builds up and that is when you start to think, "What am I doing here, why don't I go back to bed?"

But when my friend comes and knocks on the window you remember that there are plenty of other runners — in other towns or countries — who are out training at the same time and who are all aiming to beat you in the summer. The mental vision of the likes of Steve Ovett, Sebastian Coe, Steve Cram, Peter Elliott and Garry Cook all out on the streets of their home towns, flogging their guts out, is usually enough to get the negative thoughts out of my head.

After I've finished the run I'll shower and then dash off to college, which I attend between 9am and 5pm. If possible, I'll have a nap during my dinner break. There have been times when I've been so tired I've slept right through until 6pm, which is when my second training session of the day is due.

The evening session can vary from track running to gym work to road running. You may still be tired from the morning run, but you can't afford to miss it. After I come home, I'll make something to eat and then do some work, if there's time, or if not I'll just go to bed. That's it: my day from October through to May.

It can be very hard. The accumulation of all the winter workload builds up and you tend to feel fatigued all of the time. You're always feeling heavy, tired, or drained. There isn't a week in the winter I can look back on during which I can recall feeling great. But you have to go through all of that if you want the results in the summer. You just can't forgo the hard work.'

The big race

'The day of the 1982 Commonwealth Games 800m final in Brisbane would be a good one to describe. Any race day in the summer is a completely different kettle of fish to any day in winter, but a big championships — the biggest race of the whole year — intensifies everything. You tend to be on a knife-edge all of the time, but at the

Chris McGeorge

Moorcroft on the long road to the top.

same time you're very fresh and full of excess energy.

Everything is channelled towards 1 minute 45 seconds of running. Getting it right mentally at that time is very important. If you look back through the history of major championships, many great runners have buckled under pressure. You have to concen-trate on the job in hand, otherwise a whole year's work has been wasted. You might not win, of course, but you know that if you don't approach the race properly you will not do yourself justice. Everything pulls together, both mentally and physically, as you approach the peak of the whole year.

On the day of the final I had a lie-in until 9am before getting up and having breakfast with my room-mate, Tim Hutchings, the 5,000m runner. He reassured me that there was nothing to worry about and that I would do well. It may seem a bit bland and insignificant, but that does you the world of good when your nerves are beginning to jangle.

As the race was not due to be held until the late afternoon I had a good breakfast — fruitjuice, cornflakes and scrambled eggs. Diet may also seem an unimportant thing on such a big day, but when you are running abroad in an international race you have to be extremely careful about what you eat. Tummy bugs and overeating have cost a lot of good runners medals over the years. It's best to stick to the kind of food you would have at home, if at all possible.

After breakfast I went back to bed for a while, then sorted out my kit and went down to the stadium. After reporting to the officials, I went off to the warm-up track. It is in the warm-up area, where your rivals are warming up around you, that the nerves can start to destroy your composure. But you can use the nerves to your advantage in a situation like that — if you forget about the others, even if they happen to include John Walker, a former Olympic champion and world record holder. You have to use the adrenalin to pump yourself into a controlled and confident state.

The mental preparation is, at this stage, more important than the physical warm-up, which consisted of a one-mile jog followed by some stretching exercises and some striding. Then all of the finalists were marched into the stadium. We all stripped off our tracksuits, put on our spikes and started getting ready for the start. When I heard the words "on your marks" I felt good. I knew I was ready.

I remember the gun going and saying to myself "let's go out and do it; let's do the job you've come to do!" One and a half minutes later I knew I was going to finish third. Peter Bourke, of Australia, and Kenya's James Maina had a lead on me coming off the final bend and I just couldn't claw back the distance before the tape.

My immediate feeling when I crossed the line was one of disappointment. I've seen the race on video and when I finished I instinctively banged the palm of my hand against my head, as if to say "you've blown it". I thought I could have won it. Not everybody wants a bronze medal — it was a bit of an anti-climax, to be honest. A whole year's work ending up with the third-best reward wasn't totally satisfying. But, upon reflection, I can't complain about winning a medal in my first major championships. Not too many runners have done that.

Afterwards I went for a little walk on my own, just to sort things out in my own mind. I'd been to the press conference and wasn't asked one question, which only emphasised the disappointment of not winning. So I went back to my room and threw the medal in my bag.

Tim, my room-mate, came in and congratulated me and asked to see the medal, which made me feel happier. We went out to the pictures, came home, and went to bed. That was it: my first major championships final ,and the end of a year of hard training.

Result

1 P. Bourke (Australia)
   1min 45.18sec
2 J. Maina (Kenya)
   1min 45.45sec
3 C. McGeorge (GB)
   1min 45.60sec
4 J. Walker (NZ)
   1min 46.23sec

Venues

Crystal Palace

The Crystal Palace track at the National Sports Centre in South London is firmly established as the home of British athletics. It took over that role in the early 1970s when attendances began to slump at the White City stadium in West London. The first full-house of 17,000 turned up for the August Bank Holiday fixture between Britain and West Germany in 1971.

Although 'the Palace' is the home of the AAA championships and of Britain's leading international matches, the most popular meeting it hosts is the annual IAC-Coca Cola invitation evening which brings an end to the top class British season in front of sell-out crowds. After the re-surfacing of the synthetic track, which had originally been layed in 1968, it staged the Europa cup final in August 1983.

Meadowbank stadium

Since staging the highly successful 1970 Commonwealth Games, Edinburgh's Meadowbank stadium has become Britain's secondary athletics venue. That position was underlined when the stadium hosted the 1973 Europa cup final, the first time the event had come to Britain. It staged the first ever IAAF permit meeting (participation money allowed to be paid to athletes) in June 1983, and is due to host the Commonwealth Games again in 1986.

Gateshead

In 1973 Gateshead stadium was little more than a dirt track, which found difficulty in attracting local athletics events. But Brendan Foster took over as the town's sports and recreation manager that year and marked the opening of a new synthetic track in August 1974 by setting a world 3,000m record at the inaugural Gateshead games.

Crystal Palace

Since then the stadium has staged many top international fixtures, including the IAAF Golden 5,000m race in June 1981, which was fittingly won by a Gateshead Harrier, Barry Smith. Gateshead also stages an annual international cross-country event on the Riverside Park Bowl course, adjacent to the stadium, and the IAAF World cross-country championships were held there in March 1983.

Other British venues

The increase in the number of synthetic tracks which have been installed around Britain in recent years has led to the emergence of other significant athletics venues. The vastly-improved facilities at Birmingham's Alexander Park stadium, as well as its central position, have helped it to become the venue for several top fixtures during the 1983 season. Cwmbran in South Wales has also staged a number òf top meetings since the mid-1970s. The home of Britain's indoor season is at RAF Cosford, near Wolverhampton.

Gateshead Stadium: Brendan Foster points the way (All-Sport).

Bislett

It is more than a shade ironic that the Bislett stadium in Oslo has been the scene for many of the highlights of recent British athletics history. The world-famous stadium — with its tight bends, compact six-lane track and enthusiastic crowds — has become the perfect stage for setting world records — 37 were set there between 1924 and 1982 — and the most memorable of all was Dave Moorcroft's 5,000m record in 1982. His time of 13 minutes 00.42 seconds was 20 seconds faster than his previous best for the 12½ lap distance and almost 6 seconds inside the previous world record, which was held by Kenya's Henry Rono, who finished half a lap behind Coventry's Moorcroft.

The stadium has also witnessed the

main 'bouts' in the curious arms length battle between Sebastian Coe and Steve Ovett for world middle distance supremacy. Coe has set world records at 800m, 1,000m (twice) and the mile on the Scandinavian track; Ovett set 1500m and mile records there before the Moscow Olympics in 1980.

Other European venues

The growth of the European circuit since the late 1970s has led to the emergence of many other leading European venues, including: Koblenz, in West Germany, where Ovett set his world 1500m record in 1981; Zurich, where Coe broke the metric mile record in 1979; and the Heysel

Brisbane '82: the setting for the most recent Commonwealth Games.

Stadium in Brussels, home of the Ivo Van Damme memorial meeting, in which Coe set his mile record of 3 minutes 47.33 seconds in 1981.

Los Angeles

The Los Angeles Coliseum, which will host the 1984 Olympics, staged the highly successful 1932 Games. Built in 1923, the amphitheatre-like stadium is notoriously windy, which could ruin the chances of any legal sprinting and jumping records in the 1984 Games.

Los Angeles, of course, also has some of the most polluted air in the world and that is bound to affect distance runners — in particular the marathon competitors. There is even a joke circulating that the smog and permanent traffic congestion in Los Angeles will make it hard for competitors to get from their living accommodation to the Coliseum and other centres of competition. A new Rekortan synthetic track was laid at the stadium in 1983.

Los Angeles, site of the 1984 Olympics (All-Sport).

57

People in the media

The temptation to accuse a television commentator of 'not knowing what he is talking about' is often strong, and sometimes justified. The next time you feel the urge to level such criticism at a television commentator, however, it would only be fair to consider the wealth of practical knowledge and experience held by the BBC and ITV commentary teams.

BBC
David Coleman's voice has described many of the world's greatest athletic moments on TV and, while he does not have the same kind of practical experience of top class athletics as his colleagues, his interest in the sport has firm roots. At the age of 23 he won the Manchester Mile in 1949 and, three years later, his eighty-ninth placing in the English National Cross-country championships helped Manchester A and CC win bronze team medals.

Brendan Foster, a recent addition to the BBC commentary team, was arguably Britain's most popular athlete of the 1970s. The tenacious Gateshead Harrier's finest achievement was winning the 5,000m gold medal in storming fashion at the 1974 European championships in Rome. He took the bronze 10,000m gold medal two years later at the Montreal Olympics, where he also set the Games record for 5,000m. He crowned a glittering running career by capturing the Commonwealth 10,000m crown in 1978. He is the UK managing director of Nike, the world's leading running shoe manufacturers.

A former teacher and all-round athlete, **Ron Pickering** made his reputation as a leading international coach when he plucked Lynn Davies from obscurity and turned him into the 1964 Olympic long jump champion (no other British athlete had previously won an Olympic gold medal in a field event). Ron, then the Welsh

David Coleman (BBC).

58

Brendan Foster

national coach, has since become a leading sports commentator and also a consultant in planning and recreation management. He is the president of one of Britain's leading clubs, Haringey AC, and has been in the vanguard of attempts to create another much-needed indoor athletics track in Britain. He is married to Jean Desforges, winner of the women's long jump at the 1954 European championships, and their son Shaun is one of Britain's leading hammer throwers.

Like Pickering, **Stuart Storey** has also coached one of Britain's greatest ever field event athletes: Geoff Capes, the double Commonwealth shot put champion who has won more British vests than any other athlete. Formerly one of Britain's top 110m hurdlers (and an arch-rival of ITV commentator Alan Pascoe), Stuart ran for Britain in the 1968 Mexico Olympics and in the European championships in Athens the following year. A senior lecturer at Thames Polytechnic, he maintains his top-class coaching links by helping Daley Thompson with his hurdling training.

ITV
The 'front man' of ITV's athletics team and the Head of Channel 4's sports coverage, **Adrian Metcalfe** rocked the British athletics scene by setting a UK 400m record of 45.8 seconds at the age of nineteen in July 1961 — only nine months after taking up the event.

Ron Pickering

People in the media/2

Adrian Metcalfe (Channel Four).

Alan Pascoe

The precocious young Yorkshireman with the prodigious stride (up to 9ft 6ins when in full flight) had the athletics world at his feet. But illness and injury plagued his senior career and his best major international championship showing was fourth in the 400m at the 1962 European championships. He did, however, collect silver medals in Britain's 4 x 400m relay teams at the 1962 European championships and at the 1964 Olympic Games in Tokyo.

Alan Pascoe also played a major part in some great 4 x 400m relay performances by British teams: second in the 1972 Olympics, second in the Commonwealth Games and first in the European championships in 1974. But, unlike Metcalfe, he also tasted the joy of individual success at major championships. Despite failing to win an Olympic medal in an individual event, Pascoe was one of Britain's most successful athletes — a remarkable achievement for an asthmatic who failed to make his house team at his Portsmouth school.

His major championships individual medal haul was certainly impressive: 1969 European indoor championships — first 50m hurdles; 1969 European championships — third 110m hurdles; 1971 European championships — second 110m hurdles; 1974 Commonwealth Games — first 400m hurdles; 1974 European championships — first 400m hurdles; 1978 Commonwealth Games — third 400m hurdles. Alan, who is married to Della James, a former British women's 100m record holder, also won a total of 13 AAA titles.

Statistics

Olympic Records

Men

100m	9.95sec	J. Hines	US	1968
200m	19.83sec	T. Smith	US	1968
400m	43.86sec	L. Evans	US	1968
800m	1min 43.50sec	A. Juantorena	Cuba	1976
1500m	3min 34.91sec	K. Keino	Kenya	1968
3,000m steeplechase	8min 08.02sec	A. Garderud	Sweden	1976
5,000m	13min 20.24sec	B. Foster	GB	1976
10,000m	27min 38.35sec	L. Viren	Finland	1972
Marathon	2hr 09min 55sec	W. Cierpinski	East Germany	1976
110m hurdles	13.24sec	R. Milburn	US	1972
400m hurdles	47.63sec	E. Moses	US	1976
20km walk	1hr 23min 36sec	M. Damilano	Italy	1980
50km walk	3hr 49min 24sec	H. Gauder	East Germany	1980
4 x 100m	38.19sec	US		1972
4 x 400m	2min 56.16sec	US		1968
High jump	2.36m	G. Wessig	East Germany	1980
Pole vault	5.78m	W. Kozakiewicz	Poland	1980
Long jump	8.90m	R. Beamon	US	1968
Triple jump	17.39m	V. Saneyeev	USSR	1968
Shot	21.35m	V. Kiselyev	USSR	1980
Discus	68.28m	M. Wilkins	US	1976
Hammer	81.80m	Y. Syedikh	USSR	1980
Javelin	94.58m	M. Nemeth	Hungary	1976
Decathlon	8,617pts	B. Jenner	US	1976

Women

100m	11.01sec	A. Richter	West Germany	1976
200m	22.03sec	B. Wockel	East Germany	1980
400m	48.88sec	M. Koch	East Germany	1980
800m	1min 53.43sec	N. Olizaryenko	USSR	1980
1500m	3min 56.56sec	T. Kazankina	USSR	1980
100m hurdles	12.56sec	V. Komisova	USSR	1980
4 x 100m	41.60sec	East Germany		1980
4 x 400m	3min 19.23sec	East Germany		1976
High jump	1.97m	S. Simeoni	Italy	1980
Long jump	7.06m	T. Kolpakova	USSR	1980
Shot	22.41m	T. Slupianek	East Germany	1980
Discus	69.96m	E. Jahl	East Germany	1980
Javelin	68.40m	M. Colon	Cuba	1980
Pentathlon	5,083pts	N. Tkachenko	USSR	1980

World Records

Men

100m	9.93sec	C. Smith	US	1983
200m	19.72sec	P. Mennea	Italy	1979
400m	43.86sec	L. Evans	US	1968
800m	1min 41.73sec	S. Coe	GB	1981

61

Statistics/2

1500m	3min 30.77sec	S. Ovett	GB	1983
Mile	3min 47.33sec	S. Coe	GB	1981
3000m	7min 32.1sec	H. Rono	Kenya	1978
5000m	13min 00.42sec	D. Moorcroft	GB	1982
10,000m	27min 22.4sec	H. Rono	Kenya	1978
Marathon	2hrs 08min 13sec	A. Salazar	US	1982
3000m steeplechase	8min 05.4sec	H. Rono	Kenya	1978
110m hurdles	12.93sec	R. Nehemiah	US	1981
400m hurdles	47.02sec	E. Moses	US	1983
4 x 100m	37.86sec	US		1983
4 x 400m	2min 56.16sec	US		1968
High jump	2.38m	Z. Jian Hua	China	1983
Pole vault	5.83m	T. Vigneron	France	1983
Long jump	8.90m	R. Beamon	US	1968
Triple jump	17.89m	J. de Oliveira	Brazil	1975
Shot	22.22m	U. Beyer	East Germany	1983
Discus	71.86m	Y. Dumchev	USSR	1983
Hammer	84.14m	S. Litvinov	USSR	1983
Javelin	99.72m	T. Petranoff	US	1983
Decathlon	8,777pts	J. Hingsen	West Germany	1983

Women

100m	10.79sec	E. Ashford	US	1983
200m	21.71sec	M. Koch	East Germany	1979
400m	47.99sec	J. Kratochvilova	Czechoslovakia	1983
800m	1min 53.28sec	J. Kratochvilova	Czechoslovakia	1983
1500m	3min 52.47sec	T. Kazankina	USSR	1980
Mile	4min 17.44sec	M. Puica	Romania	1982
3000m	8min 26.78sec	S. Ulmasova	USSR	1982
5000m	15min 08.26sec	M. Decker	US	1982
10,000m	31min 27.57sec	R. Sadreydinova	USSR	1983
Marathon	2hrs 22min 43sec	J. Benoit	US	1983
100m hurdles	12.36sec	G. Rabsztyn	Poland	1980
400m hurdles	54.02sec	A. Ambrozene	USSR	1983
4 x 100m	41.53sec	East Germany		1983
4 x 400m	3min 19.04sec	East Germany		1982
High jump	2.04m	T. Bykova	USSR	1983
Long jump	7.43m	A. Cusmir	Romania	1983
Shot	22.45m	I. Slupianek	East Germany	1980
Discus	73.26m	G. Savinkova	USSR	1983
Javelin	74.76m	T. Lillak	Finland	1983
Heptathlon	6,836pts	R. Neubert	East Germany	1983

World Champions 1983

Men

100m	C. Lewis (US)	10.07sec
200m	C. Smith (US)	20.14sec
400m	B. Cameron (Jamaica)	45.05sec
800m	W. Wülbeck (FRG)	1min 43.65sec
1500m	S. Cram (GB)	3min 41.59sec
3,000m steeplechase	P. Ilg (FRG)	8min 15.06sec
5,000m	E. Coghlan (Ireland)	13min 28.53sec
10,000m	A. Cova (Italy)	28min 01.04sec
Marathon	R. de Castella (AUS)	2hr 10min 03sec
110m hurdles	G. Foster (US)	13.42sec
400m hurdles	E. Moses (US)	47.50sec
4 x 100m	US	37.86sec
4 x 400m	USSR	3min 0.78sec
20km walk	E. Canto (Mexico)	1hr 20min 49sec
50km walk	R. Weigel (GDR)	3hr 43min 08sec
High jump	G. Avdeenko (USSR)	2.32m
Pole vault	S. Bubka (USSR)	5.70m
Long jump	C. Lewis (US)	8.55m
Triple jump	Z. Hoffman (Poland)	17.42m
Shot	E. Sarvl (Poland)	21.39m
Discus	I. Bugar (TCH)	67.72m
Hammer	S. Litvinov (USSR)	82.68m
Javelin	D. Michel (GDR)	89.48m
Decathlon	D. Thompson (GB)	8,666pts

Women

100m	M. Göhr (GDR)	10.97sec
200m	M. Koch (GDR)	22.13sec
400m	J. Kratochvilova (TCH)	47.99sec
800m	J. Kratochvilova (TCH)	1min 54.68sec
1500m	M. Decker (US)	4min 0.90sec
3,000m	M. Decker (US)	8min 34.62sec
Marathon	G. Waitz (Norway)	2hr 28min 09sec
100m hurdles	B. Jahn (GDR)	12.35sec
400m hurdles	E. Fesenko (USSR)	54.14sec
4 x 100m	GDR	41.76sec
4 x 400m	GDR	3min 19.73sec
High jump	T. Bykova (USSR)	2.01m
Long jump	H. Daute (GDR)	7.27m
Shot	M. Fibingerova (TCH)	21.05m
Discus	M. Opitz (GDR)	68.94m
Javelin	T. Lillak (Finland)	70.82m
Heptathlon	R. Neubert (GDR)	6,714pts

Note:	FRG	West Germany
	GDR	East Germany
	TCH	Czechoslovakia
	AUS	Australia

Acknowledgements

Acknowledgements
We are most grateful to Chris McGeorge for his help in compiling this book.

Further reading
History of British Athletics by Mel Watman (Robert Hale, 1968); also *Encyclopedia of Track and Field Athletics (1964)*.
Complete Book of Athletics by Tom McNab (Ward Lock, 1980).
Official Centenary History of AAA by Peter Lovesey (Guinness Superlatives, 1979).
The Olympic Games edited by Lord Killanin and John Rodda (Macdonald & Jane, 1976).